Genealogy Business Blueprint

Turn Your Passion for Ancestry into a Profit

Table of Contents

Chapter 1. Introduction

Delve into the world of the past and capitalize on your curiosities with our Special Report: "Genealogy Business Blueprint: Turn Your Passion for Ancestry into a Profit". This is no humdrum reading material; it's an open door to transform your passionate hobby into a fruitful endeavor. This comprehensive guide is teeming with compact yet compelling information, fabulous tools, learned techniques, and indispensable tips and tricks for both novices and seasoned genealogists alike. Starting a business has never been so exciting – reminding us it's not about pursuing money, but chasing after what you love! Don't miss this opportunity to breathe life into your passion; the past has never been so present!

Chapter 2. Understanding Genealogy: The Why and How

Genealogy is a field that combines the detective work of uncovering the past with the personal joy of discovering one's own roots. It's a field full of surprises, intricacies, and revelations, often revealing more about ourselves than we had ever hoped to know.

2.1. The Importance of Genealogy

Whether you intend to turn your skills and passion for genealogy into a business or simply want to deepen your understanding of this fascinating field, it's crucial to grasp its significance. Tracing the roots of your ancestry not only uncovers your family history but also sheds light on your identity—how your ancestors' experiences, struggles, triumphs, and decisions have shaped who you are today.

Genealogy is more than simply creating a family tree; it's a journey through history. It allows you to explore your ancestors' pasts, learn about their lives, understand the times in which they lived, and even pays homage to their contributions and sacrifices. Ultimately, it fosters a connection between the past and the present, forging a link between strangers who share a common ancestry.

2.2. The How: Techniques and Tools for Genealogy

Undertaking the genealogical voyage necessitates certain technical skills, as well as an understanding of the tools available to you. The field has come a long way from archival research alone, as the rise of DNA testing and digitization of records has revolutionized genealogical research.

2.3. Traditional Research

Genealogy owes its roots to traditional research methods that rely heavily upon records, such as birth and death certificates, marriage licenses, census data, military records, and more. To effectively dig into the past, you need to find, analyze, interpret, and corroborate these records.

These documents may be housed in various places, including local courthouses, libraries, churches, genealogical societies, and national archives. It's important to note that accessibility can vary. While some records are open to the public, others may require special permissions or entail administrational fees for access.

2.4. Digital Research

In today's digital age, the internet is your best friend. Online resources have exploded in recent years, making it easier than ever to find ancestral information from the comfort of home. There are numerous websites, databases, forums, and social media groups dedicated to genealogy, many of which offer free access to digitalized records.

Worthy of note are genealogy-specific websites like Ancestry.com or FamilySearch.org that maintain extensive archives and tools. These resources can be beneficial to both beginners and advanced researchers, allowing you to search by name, place, and even events, thereby opening vast avenues of information at your fingertips.

2.5. DNA Research

Complementing traditional and digital research is DNA testing, a valuable tool that can validate your findings and uncover additional layers of your genealogy.

DNA testing has become a popular resource for genealogists as companies like 23andMe, AncestryDNA, and MyHeritage use genetic testing to track one's ethnicity and genetic relatives, and even estimate migration patterns of distant ancestors. It's a powerful tool that can provide a broader biological perspective to your research. However, it's important to approach these results with a critical eye, considering issues of privacy and accuracy.

2.6. Resources and Learning

To thrive in genealogy, continuous learning is essential. The field is constantly advancing, with new tools, methods, and resources emerging regularly. On this note, keeping updated with current practices, laws, digital advancements, and industrial conferences can help enhance your skills and can eventually add value to the services your genealogy business offers.

Realize the significance of your work: embracing genealogy is not just about tracing lineage; it's about preserving stories and keeping history alive. Whether you seek to transform your passion into a rewarding business or simply to start your genealogical journey, remember, the past reverberates through the present; the echoes are heard through you.

Chapter 3. Exploring the Market: Who Needs Genealogical Services?

The journey to starting a genealogy business requires an understanding of the market and understanding who needs genealogy services.

3.1. Understanding the Market

Identifying the target market for genealogy services is the key starting point for your business. In essence, the customer base for your services will be diverse, spanning different ages, backgrounds, and interests. Family historians, hobby genealogists, adoptees, and genetic genealogists are but a few of the customer groups that will require your services.

People's interest in their family histories and ethnic backgrounds has risen steeply in recent years, partly spurred by popular television programs and the rise of personalized ancestry DNA kits. Your potential clientele encompasses a wide range of individuals and groups, all united by their interest in family history.

In terms of age demographics, older adults often make up a large percentage of those interested in genealogical research, but it is by no means restricted only to them. Younger generations, especially millennials, are showing increasing interest in understanding their family history. For example, a popular gift for a landmark birthday such as 21 or 30 is often a personalized family tree or ancestry report. As a result, age is unlikely to be a limiting factor when targeting your genealogy services.

3.2. Family History Enthusiasts

One of the primary groups of people interested in genealogy services are family history enthusiasts. These individuals are on a quest to uncover their ancestral roots, learn about their family's pasts, and uncover fascinating stories from the changing tides of history. Many may have begun their journey into genealogy as a hobby, self-researching and building their family trees. However, as their trees grow and research becomes increasingly complex, they often need the help of a professional genealogist.

3.3. Royalty and Nobility

Believe it or not, royalty, nobility, and other people of high social standing are another potential group of clients. Those with aristocratic blood often have complex lineages that can span continents and centuries. Ascertaining the veracity of claims to titles or ownership of historical properties often requires professional genealogical research. Therefore, providing a dedicated service to this niche may be a lucrative part of your genealogy business.

3.4. Adoptees and Their families

Genealogists often work with adoptees and their families to trace biological parents and siblings. A professional can often break through records that are sealed or difficult to track. This type of research can help empower adoptees by answering questions about their past and heritage.

3.5. Legal Needs

Certain legal proceedings may require genealogical research. For instance, probate cases, when there are disagreements over an inheritance or when no will is present, genealogists can be hired to locate living relatives and heirs. Lawyers, hence, are another potential client base to consider while strategizing for your genealogy business.

3.6. DNA Companies

Genealogical DNA testing companies can also be potential clients. These businesses often need genealogists to help interpret the genetic data they've gathered and to assist customers in understanding their test results in the context of their family history.

3.7. Educational Institutions

Educational institutions, such as schools or universities, may utilize genealogy services to create curriculum-based projects that allow students to explore their personal histories. Similarly, libraries may offer genealogy workshops or series and would require a professional genealogist's contributions.

3.8. Wrapping Up

The potential market for genealogy services is vast and varied. The key is to understand your prospective clientele's needs and how you can cater to them. Whether it's family historians trying to trace their roots, or law firms in need of heir tracing services, it's about offering specialized, professional support that meets their unique needs.

As you start your genealogy business, take the time to really understand the market. Doing so, will ensure your ability to provide relevant and effective services, increase your visibility, and ultimately lead to the success of your business. The past has never been so present, and by appreciating who needs genealogical services, you'll be all set to build a business that brings history to life in fascinating ways.

Chapter 4. Skills and Tools for the Trade: Essential Knowledge for Genealogists

If you're reading this, you have probably ignited a passion for uncovering the secrets of the past, tracing your family history, and learning the ins and outs of genealogy. The business that revolves around this passion is as intricate as it is rewarding. In order to dip your toes or to dive headlong into this business venture, it's essential to arm yourself with the right set of skills and tools. Let's find out what these are!

4.1. Essential Skills: Discover the Genealogist in You

Every genealogist needs a robust set of skills. Don't worry; these are less about natural talent and more about learning, practicing, and becoming adept.

4.1.1. Attention to Detail: The Devil is in the Detail

The first key skill for any genealogist is attention to detail. The ability to provide a thorough examination of every document looked at is imperative. You'll find names, dates, locations, relationships, and a host of additional information lurking in the corners of every record. Some details may initially appear irrelevant, but they may turn out to be crucial clues later in your research.

4.1.2. Analytical Skill: Fact-finding and Interpretation

You'll be collating a lot of data and information in your research work; it's an analytical skill that will help you make connections between different sets of information. With keen analytical ability, you can interpret data better and build accurate family trees. This skill will also enable you to differentiate between facts, hypothesis, and assumption, all of which will be intermingled in your findings.

4.1.3. Persistence: Patience in Pursuit

Due to the nature of this work, persistence is quite necessary; it can sometimes be a treasure hunt without a map. Records are scattered far and wide, in different formats, and at times, cryptic to understand. A substantial portion of your work may also rely on public cooperation, which could be challenging. But remember, the most rewarding discoveries often come after a long process of relentless searching.

4.1.4. Communication Skills: Reach Out with Effect

As much as genealogy is about scouring through old records, it's also about reaching out to people. These could be family members or strangers who would be sharing personal and sensitive information. Hence, it's essential to approach your interviews and conversations with delicacy, respect, and exceptional persuasion and listening skills.

4.2. Essential Tools: The Genealogist's Arsenal

Empowering yourself with the right tools can significantly simplify your genealogy business journey. Here are some must-have tools that every genealogist should be well-acquainted with.

4.2.1. Computers and Genealogical Software

In this digital age, having a computer is not a luxury but a necessity. You'll be sorting massive amounts of data which would warrant the need for a computer, along with genealogical software tools. Numerous software programs allow you to construct family trees, record your findings, gather historical data, and back up all your precious research data safely.

4.2.2. Internet Access

It's essential to have regular access to the internet, considering the wealth of online resources and databases available for genealogists. Websites, digital archives, and online networks can prove invaluable in tracking down information about individuals and family histories worldwide.

4.2.3. Access to Ancestry Databases

There are several popular ancestry databases available today, each housing billions of historical records. Websites such as Ancestry.com, FamilySearch.org, and MyHeritage.com, among others, should be bookmarked on your browser. Subscription-based or free, these are the key tools for any passionate genealogist.

4.2.4. DNA Testing Kits

Genetic genealogy, using DNA testing, has been instrumental in unraveling family histories. Different kinds of DNA testing kits, like Y-DNA, mtDNA, or Autosomal DNA testing kits, can help trace different parts of your ancestry. Not only can they confirm existing paths on your tree but also prompts new discoveries.

4.2.5. Reference Books and Maps

While the world is going digital, traditional reference books and maps still play a critical role in genealogy research by providing a wealth of information that may not be available online. Historical atlases can give insight into boundary changes over time, while guidebooks can provide details on available resources and how to access them.

This is an overture to the world of genealogy business; a field where the detective work of connecting lineage dots marries the academic diligence of historic research. The potent combination of the discussed skills and tools can set you up for an enriching journey of tracing lineages, uncovering family histories, and satisfying your relentless curiosity. Remember, your passion makes this business unique, and the meticulous training and preparation make you unique in this business.

Chapter 5. Step-by-step Guide: Setting Up Your Genealogy Business

Before venturing into any business, detailed planning and preparation is required. Your genealogy business is no exception. This section will guide you through the necessary steps to setting up your business, equipped with vital principles and best practices to help you start strong and succeed.

5.1. Decide on Your Business Model

There are many ways you can structure your genealogy business. Some people offer services as independent consultants, while others create online platforms where clients can explore their family history. Decide whether you want to focus on:

1. Researching genealogical records and creating family trees
2. Offering workshops and trainings for amateur genealogists
3. Selling genealogical charts, tools and software
4. Creating an online database of genealogical records for subscription

Your decision should be based on your expertise and the market demand. Research what's already available and find a niche for yourself where you can provide unique value.

5.2. Write Your Business Plan

Outline what you hope to achieve with your business and how you plan to do it. This will serve as your guide as you set up and run your business.

1. Executive Summary: A brief overview of your business.

2. Company Description: The ins and outs of your genealogy business.

3. Market Analysis: Survey of your potential customers and competitors in the industry.

4. Organization and Management: Your business structure and management team.

5. Service or Product Line: Detailed description of your services or products.

6. Marketing and Sales Strategy: How you plan to attract and retain customers.

7. Financial Projections: Your projected income and expenses for the next three to five years.

5.3. Register Your Business

Ensure your business is legally compliant:

1. Choose a Business Name: Be creative but clear about the services you provide.

2. Register Your Business: Register your business at the local county or state office.

3. Get Federal and State Tax IDs: Apply for a Federal Employer Identification Number (FEIN) from the IRS. Your state might also require a separate tax ID.

4. Apply for Licenses and Permits: Ensure that you have all necessary licenses and permits.

5.4. Create Your Business Website

A website is essential for reaching potential clients. It acts as a platform to advertise your services, showcase your work, and provide opportunities for clients to contact you.

1. Choose a Suitable Platform: Platforms such as WordPress, Wix, or Squarespace are excellent choices for building a professional-looking website.

2. Design Your Website: Ensure that your website is user-friendly and visually appealing.

3. Keep Your Website Updated: Regularly update your website with helpful articles, recent works, customer reviews, and other relevant content.

5.5. Develop Your Services and Pricing

Create detailed descriptions of your services and decide how much you will charge for them.

1. Set Your Objectives: Clarify what you'll do for the client and what the final product will look like.

2. Decide Your Pricing: Consider the complexity of the work, the time it will take, and what your competitors are charging.

5.6. Market Your Business

Now that you've established your business, it's time to attract clients:

1. Identify Your Target Audience: Understand who they are, their needs, where they are, and how to reach them.

2. Create a Marketing Strategy: This can involve online marketing,

direct mail, attending local events, or a combination of these.

3. Use Social Media: Platforms such as Facebook, LinkedIn, and Instagram can help you connect with potential clients and build your brand.

Setting up your own genealogy business is a significant step, one that brings your passion to life. Remember, success won't happen overnight. It will require dedication, patience, and the continuous eagerness to learn and grow. As you embark on this rewarding journey, know that the past is serving you, shaping the foundation of a business that has the potential to thrive in the present as well as in the future. It's not just a business about tracing ancestry; it's about providing a valuable service that helps people grasp their past as they navigate their present and future.

Chapter 6. Strategies for Success: Marketing Your Business and Building a Brand

Understanding how to properly market your business and establish a brand identity is vital for the success of your genealogy enterprise. To succeed in the genealogy industry, you must carefully craft and execute strategies that will get your brand noticed and nurture prospects into loyal, paying customers.

6.1. Develop a Unique Value Proposition

Your unique value proposition (UVP) is essentially the cornerstone of your branding and marketing efforts. It's what sets your genealogy business apart from competitors. Your UVP tells potential customers why they should conduct business with you instead of your competitors. Identifying your UVP requires a deep understanding of your business, the market, and customer needs.

Firstly, it's essential to analyze what kind of services competitors are offering and identify potential gaps or unmet customer needs. You should look into how they are operations, their pricing, and their customer service policies.

Secondly, consider the strengths of your genealogy business. What are you doing differently or better? Maybe you offer a uniquely comprehensive range of records, or perhaps you offer customized reports that include a more persona-centric narrative of an individual's ancestors.

Lastly, discuss with your target customers. Ask them about their experiences with competitor services. Find out what they like, what they don't like, and what they would love to see in a genealogy service.

6.2. Branding Your Business

A strong brand is more than just a logo or a tagline; it's a whole sensory experience that seeks to create positive associations and customer loyalty.

Your brand should be reflective of your UVP and should embody the values you want your business to represent. A carefully thought out brand strategy can influence your potential customers in subtle yet effective ways, and ultimately sway their decision to choose your service over any other.

To create a compelling brand: 1. Choose a business name that is both meaningful and memorable. 2. Design a logo that is simple, versatile, and relevant. 3. Match your visual and textual elements such as colors, typography, and taglines to the feelings and impressions you want your brand to invoke. 4. Ensure consistency in all your communications. 5. Use storytelling to foster a deeper connection with your audience.

6.3. Market Research

Market research is a vital component of your marketing strategy. It involves gathering, recording, and analyzing information about your customers, competitors, and the industry at large.

Market research helps in:

- Identifying and understanding your target market.
- Understanding customer needs and wants.

- Spotting business trends.

- Identifying potential areas for growth.

- Making informed decisions about the development of your products/services.

Different types of market research techniques that can be used include surveys, focus groups, observation, and interviews among others. You can either do this research yourself or hire a market research firm to do it for you.

6.4. Designing a Marketing Plan

Your marketing plan outlines your overall game plan for how you'll find and retain clients. It's an essential road map for your business success.

Your marketing plan should cover:

1. SWOT Analysis: Identify Your Strengths, Weaknesses, Opportunities, and Threats.

2. Marketing Goals: Set clear, attainable, and measurable goals.

3. Target Audience: Identify who you're targeting.

4. Marketing Budget: Determine how much you can spend.

5. Marketing Channels: Decide which channels to use.

6.5. Utilizing Digital Marketing

In this digital age, it's imperative that genealogy businesses leverage different digital marketing tactics, platforms, and strategies. Digital marketing offers unique opportunities for small businesses to reach out to more potential clients within their budget range.

Some effective digital marketing strategies include:

1. SEO (Search Engine Optimization): This helps your website rank higher in search engine results, which improves its visibility.

2. Content Marketing: This involves creating and sharing online materials that don't necessarily directly promote your genealogy business but stimulate interest in its products or services.

3. Social Media Marketing: Use platforms like Facebook, Twitter, LinkedIn, and Instagram to reach out to people and get your brand noticed.

4. Email Marketing: Use email to nurture prospective customers, offer them attractive deals, or to keep in touch with past clients.

6.6. Networking and Collaboration

Establish relationships with other businesses or individuals who can refer customers to you. Look for complementary businesses that service the same target market but offer non-competing services.

Remember, the journey towards building a successful genealogy business is rigorous, but with meticulous planning, a bit of creativity, and persistence, you can create a profitable business and help many individuals connect with their heritage and enrich their lives. There's no better time than now to breathe life into your passion for unraveling the past, making it your present, and shaping your future with it.

Chapter 7. Unearthing Revenue Streams: Ways to Monetize Your Genealogical Skills

Embarking on the journey of turning your genealogy skills into a business can be exhilarating. However, understanding how to monetise your unique set of skills is crucial to sustainable success. This venture can take many forms - whether you're tracing family histories, reconstructing ancestral regions, or helping people understand their genetic profiles.

7.1. Consulting Services

One of the first ways you can turn your genealogical skills into a business opportunity is by offering consulting services. Many people are interested in their family histories but lack the expertise or time to conduct all the necessary research. They are willing to pay for an expert consultant to uncover their roots and create a detailed family tree.

As a genealogy consultant, you might find yourself combing through birth records, death certificates, marriage licenses, and more. You'll trace lineage back through generations, uncovering hidden stories and family secrets along the way. Services can range from basic family tree generation to deep, comprehensive dives into a family's past and their geographical origins.

7.2. Producing Informative Content

In the digital age, knowledge is highly valuable. A popular way to monetize your genealogy skills is by producing informative content. This venture can take various forms:

Writing Articles or Blog Posts: You might write articles or blog posts about genealogy for various publications. Whether it's sharing how to get started with genealogy, explaining different research techniques or providing tips for overcoming common challenges, your expert knowledge can be used to create compelling, sought-after content.

Creating eBooks or Guides: Another option is creating in-depth eBooks or guides on genealogical research. Done right, these can be a solid source of passive income.

Teaching Online Courses: Platforms like Udemy, Skillshare, or Coursera allow experts to create courses around their specialities. Leveraging these platforms, you can create detailed genealogy courses and sell them to interested students.

Starting a Podcast or YouTube Channel: Audio-visual content is rapidly growing in popularity. Starting a podcast or YouTube channel about genealogy can help you reach a broader audience.

7.3. Genetic Genealogy Testing Services

The rise in popularity of genetic testing is an exciting opportunity for genealogy businesses. People who want to know more about their heritage often turn to genetics for answers. As a genealogist with a solid understanding of genetics, you can offer genetic genealogy testing assistance - helping people interpret their test results and connect them with their ancestral past.

7.4. Selling Genealogy Products

There's a strong demand for a variety of genealogy products. From family tree posters to genealogy software, the potential for creating and selling genealogy-related items is significant. You might design your personalised genealogy charts, or create unique, genealogy-centric gifts.

7.5. Professional Speaking and Workshops

As you establish your expertise in the field, opportunities to speak at seminars, workshops, conferences, and other events may come your way. These speaking gigs not only further establish you as an expert in your field but can also prove to be lucrative.

7.6. Hosting Genealogy Tours

If you live near or have access to a location rich in history, consider hosting genealogy tours. These tours can provide a hands-on experience to your clients, allowing them to walk in the footsteps of their ancestors.

Building any business is a journey. It is key to have passion, but even more important to figure out how to monetize that passion for sustainable success. With this guide, you have a roadmap to potential revenue streams that allow you to make the most out of your passion for genealogy. The key is to start, refine, and remain responsive to opportunities and shifts in the market – the past, after all, can be a key to your profitable future.

Chapter 8. Building a Client Base: Networking and Relationship Management

Building a solid client base is key in turning your passion for genealogy into a profitable business. However, forming relationships and maintaining them in a business setting requires a strategic approach and strong management skills. Comprehending the interconnected components of networking and relationship management can lead you to a successful genealogy business.

8.1. Client Acquisition Strategies

Your initial customer acquisition strategy should be as much about research and learning as it is about business growth. You will need to determine what types of clients you work best with, which are most profitable for your business, and which are most likely to refer your services.

Below are some strategies to employ:

1. Ask for referrals: Tap into your personal network — friends, family, and acquaintances who already know your skill and passion for genealogy. Give these people an idea of your ideal client and ask them if they know anyone who fits the description.

2. Volunteer in local genealogical societies: Volunteering offers opportunities to showcase your skills and interact directly with people who share your interests. This could generate leads for your business.

3. Use online platforms: Websites and forums frequented by genealogy enthusiasts are potential gold mines for client acquisition. Regularly contribute valuable content to these

platforms and you can establish yourself as a credible expert.

4. Attend networking events: Go to national and international conferences, symposiums, and workshops on genealogy. These events are prime meeting spots for potential clients and collaborators.

5. Partner with related businesses: Establish relationships with businesses in related fields — history magazines, ancestry DNA testing companies, heritage travel planners, etc.

8.2. Building Relationships: The Client Journey Mapping

Understanding the journey of your client from their perspective is essential to offering them a valuable and memorable experience. Here's a simple client journey map to guide you:

1. Awareness: This is the phase where a potential client first learns about your services.

2. Consideration: Here, the potential client evaluates your services and how well they meet their needs.

3. Decision: The client chooses to invest in your services.

4. Service: You provide the service to the client, ensuring high-quality professional work.

5. Post-service: Once the project is complete, check on client satisfaction and open up possibilities for future collaboration.

8.3. Creating Customer Loyalty

Satisfied customers are more likely to refer you to others and repeat business with you. Creating customer loyalty is one of the surefire ways to build your client base. Factors that determine customer loyalty include the quality and value of the service, the customer experience, and the depth of relationship with the customer.

Here are some methods to ensure customer loyalty:

1. Deliver High-Quality Results: It goes without saying that the quality of your work should be top-tier. Customers will endure high costs or inconvenience for a service that is worth it.

2. Offer Excellent Customer Service: From timely responses to effective communication, always strive to offer the best customer service.

3. Build an Emotional Connection: Knowing your clients on a more personal level will help earn their loyalty. Connecting through shared interests or values can create strong ties.

4. Ask for Feedback: Lastly, always ask your clients for feedback post-service. This shows you care about their satisfaction and are always striving to improve.

8.4. Expanding Your Client Base: Scaling Your Business

Once a solid client base is established, it's time to scale your business. Here are several steps:

1. Invest in marketing: Now more than ever, you will need a robust marketing strategy. Boosting your online presence and investing in online and local advertisements can work well.

2. Find ways to add value: Offering additional services or a membership model for returning customers encourages loyalty and attracts new clients.

3. Seek collaboration opportunities: Partnering with other businesses or genealogists for bigger projects can diversify your income streams.

In conclusion, building a client base in a genealogy business involves a well-rounded strategy encompassing acquisition, relationship building, loyalty, and expansion. Networking and relationship management skills are vital in this journey, allowing you to connect with a wide variety of potential clients and pleasing them with high-quality service.

Chapter 9. Bridging the Gap: Translating Technical Jargon for Your Clients

In the realm of genealogy, it is imperative to remove any barriers to communication between you and your clients. This requires the translation of technical jargon into everyday language that anyone can grasp, thus bridging the gap between the genealogist and the client. Here, we will explore the practical ways and methods to make this possible.

9.1. Understanding the Language of Genealogy

First and foremost, it's crucial to have a detailed understanding of the terminology used in genealogy. As with any specialized field, genealogy has its language - a collection of words and phrases specific to the discipline. These include fundamental terms such as "ancestor," "descendant," and "family tree," to more complex nomenclatures like "endogamy," "pedigree collapse," and "consanguinity."

Taking out the time to familiarize yourself with these terms will help you articulate complex genealogical issues in a simpler, more accessible manner. Resources like a genealogy dictionary can bolster your vocabulary and provide you with a more holistic understanding of terminology.

9.2. Breaking Down the Jargon

Once you're well-grounded in the language of genealogy, the next step is translating this language for clients without a background in the field. A few strategies can assist you in simplifying complex terms:

- **Use Analogies**: Analogies can help illustrate complex genealogical concepts. For example, one might liken a family tree to an actual tree, with roots representing ancestors and branches symbolizing descendants. The idea is to use simple, relatable images or concepts to explain challenging ideas.

- **Break it Down**: Some genealogical concepts might need to be broken down into smaller, more understandable elements. This strategy involves articulating the intricacies of genealogy one concept at a time.

- **Use Visual Aids**: Implementing visual representations, such as charts and diagrams, can make a profound impact on understanding abstract or complicated ideas.

9.3. Communicating Effectively with Your Clients

Effective communication goes beyond understanding or even breaking down jargon; it's also about creating a dialogue that is engaging, approachable, and, most importantly, informative to your clients.

- **Use Everyday Language**: Replace any jargon or technical terms with everyday language as much as possible.

- **Engage in Active Listening**: Make sure you're not just talking at your clients but also taking the time to listen and understand their needs and questions.

- **Clarify and Repeat**: Always clarify pertinent pieces of information and repeat vital points to cement understanding.

9.4. Handling Challenges in Communication

Occasionally, you might encounter resistance or confusion from your clients when explaining complex concepts, which can be a challenge. It would be helpful to identify some common issues and strategize how best to handle them.

- **Dealing with Unfamiliarity**: If a client is entirely unfamiliar with genealogical concepts, you might need to start from the basics before moving to more complex principles.

- **Addressing Misunderstanding**: If a client misunderstands something, clarify it straight away to avoid further confusion.

- **Managing Resistance**: Sometimes a client may resist certain information due to varied reasons, including cultural or personal beliefs. It's essential to handle this with sensitivity and appropriateness.

9.5. The Importance of Compassion and Patience

Lastly, remember that genealogy deals with people's histories and can bring up strong emotions. Be patient and compassionate in your communication. You will find that being an effective communicator is not only about knowledge but also about kindness and understanding.

In the end, bridging the communication gap between you and your client will make your genealogy services more effective and rewarding—for both parties involved. The strategies outlined in this chapter provide a blueprint for accomplishing this goal. Embrace them, and watch as your client relationships deepen, and your business thrives.

Chapter 10. Getting Legal: Understanding the Laws Fabrics of Genealogy Business

Navigating legal landscapes can be convoluted and challenging. Yet, it's an absolute necessity when setting up a business of any kind, including a genealogy business. This section will equip you with the fundamental understanding and resources you need to legally structure and protect your business.

10.1. Legal Spectrum: An Overview

A genealogy business is not a one-size-fits-all endeavour. Depending on your intentions, your operations might touch various aspects of law, from privacy laws to intellectual property rights. Thus, understanding these laws and how they apply to your business model is critical.

First and foremost, always respect the privacy of living individuals when tracing family trees. Most countries have stringent data protection and privacy laws. Failure to abide by them could land you in legal trouble.

Next, understand copyright law. As a genealogist, you might utilize artifacts, records, photos, and other hereditary materials to conduct research. Always inquire about the copyright status of these materials and seek permission from the copyright owner before use.

Finally, when it comes to sharing and selling your genealogical discoveries, your obligations will depend on the format of the information and how you've acquired it. Legal guidance can be invaluable when transforming this data into usable content or services.

10.2. Selecting Your Legal Structure

One of the first decisions you will need to make within the realm of legality is deciding on your business' structure. Sole proprietorship, partnership, corporation, or limited liability company (LLC) – each has its benefits, drawbacks, and legal implications.

A *sole proprietorship* is the simplest form of business, and it's often a preferable option for genealogists who prefer to work independently. Under this structure, you and your business are legally seen as a single entity.

A *partnership*, as the name suggests, is when two or more individuals start a shared business venture. If you envision your genealogy business to be a team effort, a partnership is worth considering. But remember, you and your partner(s) are personally liable for any business debts.

A *corporation* separates the owners and the company as distinct legal entities. When the corporation makes a profit, it is first taxed at the corporate level, and if profits are distributed to owners (shareholders), they're taxed again at personal income tax rates.

Finally, an *LLC* combines elements of partnerships and corporations. Owners aren't personally financially responsible for business debts, and their personal assets are protected. Seek professional advice to decide which structure aligns best with your intended business.

10.3. Crafting Your Business Plan

While a business plan may not be a legal document, it's an essential tool for securing funding, attracting partners, and strategic planning.

The plan should be comprehensive, incorporating an executive summary, business profile, marketing strategies, operational procedures, and financial specifications.

Notably, the business plan must also address risk factors. Analysis and contingency plans for legal risks, such as breaches of privacy or copyright infringement, are a must. If you're pursuing funding, this component can be particularly crucial as it demonstrates your level of preparedness.

10.4. Licensing and Regulatory Concerns

Depending on your location and the specific services your genealogy business provides, you may require licenses or permits. Additionally, businesses often need to secure an Employer Identification Number (EIN) from the Internal Revenue Service (U.S.) or analogous authorities elsewhere. Regulations can be region-specific, so it's essential to understand the requirements in your locality.

As a genealogist, you should also consider registering with professional bodies. Although not necessarily a legal requirement, membership can boost credibility and provide access to essential resources and networks.

10.5. Intellectual Property Protection

Even though genealogical data (names, dates, facts) cannot be copyrighted, how you present and package this information potentially can. Consider protecting your website content, reports, books, methodologies, and original databases with copyrights and trademarks.

Remember, obtaining protection can be a complex process, and legal advice may be necessary to navigate it successfully. Laws can vary by country, and international IP protection often involves managing multiple jurisdictions and legal systems.

10.6. Contracts and Confidentiality Agreements

To cultivate professionalism and manage expectations, consider employing contracts when engaging clients. These legally binding agreements define the scope of services, payment terms, and contingency measures in case of disagreement.

In addition, you may need confidentiality agreements when dealing with clients' sensitive information, particularly when the genealogical work involves living individuals. These agreements can serve to legally bind you and your clients to preserve privacy and confidentiality of data.

Most critically, remember that outstanding legal issues can derail your genealogy business before it even takes off. Therefore, arm yourself with legal knowledge, remain compliant, and don't hesitate to seek professional legal advice when you're in doubt. Let the law not block but guide you in your genealogy business journey. The past requires respect, and the law ensures it!

Chapter 11. Growth and Expansion: How to Scale Your Genealogy Business

Growing as a business entity and expanding in the genealogy industry requires a thoughtful and strategic approach. From leveraging technological advancements to forming valuable partnerships, every choice you make can significantly influence your success trajectory.

11.1. Understanding the Genealogy Market

Understanding your market is the first step towards expanding your business. Begin your exploration with the following areas:

- The demographic profile of your clients such as their age, ethnicity, income level and educational background.

- The reasons why clients are interested in genealogy services. This can include a sense of identity, family medical history, or curiosity.

- Identify the geographical location of the clients. Online tools can enable you to reach genealogy enthusiasts from around the world.

- The competitive landscape within the genealogy industry including both direct and indirect competition.

By identifying patterns within the genealogy market, you can make informed strategical decisions to refine your services and meet your audience's needs more effectively.

11.2. Utilizing Technology to Accelerate Growth

Software advancements and digital tools can substantially aid in both genealogical research and managing your business.

Genealogy software allows you to gather, organize and analyze ancestral data more efficiently, and cloud-based platforms enable clients to easily access and share this information. Big data tools can also be utilized to study vast amounts of data and discover complex patterns.

While free platforms can serve beginners in the field, investing in state-of-the-art software can improve your processing speed and provide a more comprehensive analysis – a factor that can distinguish you from your competitors.

Apart from genealogical research, technology can also be utilized for business activities. Consider investing in a powerful CRM software to streamline your sales process and customer interactions. An intuitive and user-friendly website can help potential clients understand your offerings, and search engine optimization (SEO) can increase your visibility online.

11.3. Building a Strong Brand

Branding is a pivotal aspect of business growth. Proper branding influences how your business is perceived by both existing and potential clients, distinguishes you from your competitors, and can even propel your business to the global stage.

Identify your unique selling proposition (USP) and communicate this through your marketing tools. Consistently use the same tone of voice, colors, and logos across your website, social media, and printed materials.

Storytelling is also an effective tool for connecting with clients on a deeper level; share the story behind your business, your passion for genealogy research, and how your services can help others discover their ancestry.

11.4. Networking and Partnerships

Forming valuable partnerships and networking can assist you in accessing a wider client base and cross-promoting your services.

Consider collaborating with heritage organizations, educational institutions, tourism boards, and fellow genealogists. Attend conferences, workshops, and forums to network with other industry professionals and potential clients.

11.5. Rethinking Pricing Strategies

As your business grows, you may need to revise your pricing strategy. While you started off with competitive pricing to gain a market foothold, as your brand becomes more established, you can consider raising your prices. Additionally, a tiered pricing model can cater to different customer segments – from beginners to advanced researchers.

11.6. Investing in Continued Learning

Keep abreast of the latest trends and advancements in the genealogy industry. Attend workshops, lectures, webinars, and enroll in certification programs if possible. Staying current will ensure you continue providing top-notch services to your clients.

11.7. Hiring and Outsourcing

As your business expands, consider hiring employees or outsourcing certain tasks. This allows you to focus on core activities, such as research and client interaction, and leave administrative or technical tasks to others.

In conclusion, scaling your genealogy business involves a multifaceted approach, involving understanding your market, leveraging technology, building a strong brand, networking, and continually investing in learning. With passion and dedication, your love for genealogy can not only yield personal satisfaction but also lucrative professional growth.